DIANNE MACK

Dialectical Behavior Therapy (DBT) Demystified

A Comprehensive Guide to Understanding and Implementing Effective Strategies for Emotional Regulation and Mindful Living

Contents

1

Chapter 1: Introduction to Dialectical Behavior Therapy (DBT)

ialectical Behavior Therapy (DBT) is a comprehensive and evidence-based therapeutic approach designed to help individuals develop effective coping strategies, regulate intense emotions, and improve interpersonal relationships. Initially developed by psychologist Dr. Marsha M. Linehan in the 1980s, DBT emerged as a specialized form of cognitive-behavioral therapy (CBT) tailored for individuals struggling with emotional dysregulation, self-destructive behaviors, and challenges in interpersonal effectiveness.

DBT is particularly renowned for its application in treating conditions such as Borderline Personality Disorder (BPD), though it has proven beneficial for various mental health concerns, including depression, anxiety, substance abuse, and eating disorders. The distinguishing feature of DBT lies in its integration of both acceptance-oriented and change-oriented strategies, creating a dialectical balance between validation and change.

The therapy draws upon a synthesis of cognitive-behavioral techniques, mindfulness principles derived from Eastern contemplative traditions, and dialectical philosophy, emphasizing the synthesis of opposing concepts. A core dialectic within DBT is the balance between acceptance of oneself and the need for change. This synthesis encourages individuals to acknowledge their current state while actively working towards positive transformation.

DBT consists of four main components:

Mindfulness Skills: Mindfulness is a central component of DBT, focusing on cultivating awareness of the present moment without judgment. Practicing mindfulness helps individuals develop emotional regulation and distress tolerance.

Interpersonal Effectiveness: This component addresses the development of effective communication, assertiveness, and relationship-building skills. Individuals learn to navigate interpersonal challenges, set boundaries, and enhance their ability to interact positively with others.

Emotion Regulation: Emotion regulation skills in DBT assist individuals in understanding, accepting, and managing their emotions effectively. Techniques include identifying and labeling emotions, reducing emotional vulnerability, and developing healthy coping mechanisms.

Distress Tolerance: DBT emphasizes the importance of learning skills to tolerate and navigate distressing situations without resorting to destructive behaviors. This component equips individuals with tools for crisis management and self-soothing techniques.

DBT is often delivered through individual therapy sessions, skills training groups, phone coaching for real-time support, and therapist consultation teams to support therapists in their work. The comprehensive nature of DBT allows individuals to address multiple facets of their lives and provides a framework for building a life worth living.

While originally developed for specific populations, the versatility of DBT has led to its adaptation for various mental health challenges. Its success lies in offering a structured yet flexible framework that combines practical skills training with a compassionate and nonjudgmental approach, fostering growth and positive change for individuals facing emotional and behavioral difficulties.

Understanding the Origins and Development of DBT

A thorough, scientifically supported treatment for borderline personality disorder (BPD) is dialectical behavior therapy (DBT). The patient populations for which DBT has the greatest empirical support are women with borderline personality disorder (BPD) who are parasuicidal; however, patients with BPD and substance use disorders (SUDs), individuals who fit the criteria for binge-eating disorder, and elderly patients who are depressed have shown encouraging results. While DBT and other cognitive-behavioral approaches share many similarities, DBT treatment requires a few essential and distinctive components. Serving the five functions of treatment, the biosocial theory and emphasizing emotions in treatment, a consistent dialectical philosophy, mindfulness and acceptance-oriented interventions are a few of these components.

Marsha Linehan developed dialectical behavior therapy (DBT) as a means of treating multiproblematic, suicidal women. After reading up on effective psychosocial interventions for other disorders, like depression, anxiety disorders, and other emotion-related problems, Linehan put together a package of cognitive-behavioral therapies that were supported by research and specifically addressed suicidal behavior. Since the initial focus of these interventions was primarily on altering behaviors and cognitions, many patients experienced feelings of invalidation, misinterpretation, and criticism. As a result, many patients stopped receiving treatment altogether.

Clinical experiences with multiproblematic, suicidal patients stimulated additional research and treatment development through a synthesis of science and practice. Most significantly, Linehan incorporated techniques into the treatment plans intended to support the patient in accepting herself, her feelings, thoughts, the outside world, and other people as well as to express acceptance of the patient. As a result, dialectical philosophy served as the cornerstone for DBT, encouraging therapists to continuously combine and balance acceptance and change-oriented techniques.

In the end, this research produced a thorough, empirically supported, cognitive-behavioral treatment for borderline personality disorder (BPD). Weekly individual therapy sessions (about one hour), weekly group skills training sessions (about 1.5–2.5 hours), and weekly team meetings for therapist consultation (about one to two hours) make up the typical DBT treatment regimen. DBT is currently an effective and targeted treatment for BPD and related issues, as shown by eight published, well-controlled, randomized clinical trials (RCTs).

This article focuses on a number of important DBT features and is structured around the main concerns that practitioners may have when choosing whether and how to use the treatment. In doing so, this article mainly focuses on what makes DBT different from other treatments in terms of theory and practice, who the ideal patient populations are, and what essential and particular components of DBT need to be present for each individual patient.

Using the Research Evidence as a Guide to Determine When to Apply DBT
Research on treatment with patients who are similar to the patient in question in terms of problem areas, diagnoses, or characteristics is a crucial consideration when determining whether to use DBT or other treatments for a specific patient. Although DBT has been used by researchers and treatment developers with a wide range of patient populations, the majority of RCTs have been conducted on individuals with BPD, primarily women. A brief summary of the well-controlled RCTs that have assessed DBT is provided in

the following section.

BPD patients who are parasuicidal. The most consistent finding for BPD patients with parasuicidal behavior is that DBT leads to superior reductions in parasuicidal behavior when compared to control conditions. In the first randomized controlled trial (RCT) of DBT, which included 44 parasuicidal women with BPD, the treatment was found to be more effective than treatment as usual (TAU), which is community-based treatment, in lowering the frequency and medical severity of parasuicide, inpatient hospitalization days, trait anger, and social functioning. During the first half of the 12-month follow-up period, DBT patients showed reduced parasuicidal behavior and anger as well as improved social adjustment. During the last half of the follow-up period, improvements in social adjustment were still observed, and DBT patients experienced fewer days of inpatient psychiatric care.

With a more stringent control condition consisting of treatment by community practitioners recognized as experts in treating BPD (treatment-by-community experts, or TBCE), the largest and most recent RCT of DBT (N=101) replicated the first study. According to this study, during the 12-month treatment and the 12-month follow-up period, DBT patients had higher reductions in psychiatric hospitalization, angry behavior, medical risk of parasuicidal behavior, suicide attempts, and ER visits than TBCE patients.

DBT has been studied in a few community settings, including a VA hospital and a community mental health center, for women with BPD. Turner6 compared a client-centered therapy control condition to a modified version of DBT that only included individual therapy in a community mental health setting. Suicidal ideation, intentional self-harm, inpatient days, impulsivity, anger, and general mental health issues were all less common among patients receiving DBT. Furthermore, compared to TAU patients, DBT patients reported higher decreases in suicidal ideation, hopelessness, depression, and anger in a study of female veterans with BPD. There is no available follow-up data for these two studies.

Addiction to drugs and BPD in women. The second patient group, consisting of women with BPD and a substance use disorder (SUD), has shown encouraging results with DBT. In the first study in this area, DBT was compared to TAU for women who met BPD and SUD8 criteria. The results showed that DBT patients had lower treatment dropout rates and demonstrated greater reductions in drug use both during the 12-month treatment and during the four-month follow-up period. In a follow-up study, women with BPD who were dependent on opiates were randomized to receive DBT or a strict control condition known as Comprehensive Validation Treatment with 12-step (CVT-12S). Participants in both conditions additionally received an opiate replacement drug called LAAM (levomethadyl acetate hydrochloride). With only acceptance-oriented interventions intended to regulate treatment access time, academic treatment setting, and therapist experience and commitment, CVT-12S was a pared-down version of DBT. During the 12-month treatment, participants in both DBT and CVT-12S demonstrated a significant decrease in opiate use; however, at the 16-month follow-up, DBT patients had more sustained abstinence from opiate use.

DBT for substance abusers with BPD has also been studied in a few RCTs conducted outside of the United States. In a recent study, standard DBT was compared to treatment-as-usual (TAU) for women with BPD and a substance use disorder (N=27) at the Centre for Addiction and Mental Health (CAMH) in Canada.10 DBT patients showed greater reductions in alcohol use and suicidal and parasuicidal behaviors, but not in drug use. Of the patients with BPD included in a Dutch study, 53% also satisfied the criteria for a substance use disorder (SUD). Results showed that, in comparison to TAU patients, DBT patients showed larger reductions in parasuicidal behavior and impulse-control problem behaviors (such as binging, gambling, and reckless driving, but not substance abuse). Over the course of the six-month follow-up period, DBT patients continued to exhibit reduced levels of impulsive behavior, parasuicidal behavior, and alcohol consumption.

Additional clinical problems and populations. Furthermore, a few studies have looked at DBT-focused therapies for various clinical issues, such as depression in senior citizens and eating disorders. When Telch and colleagues compared a wait list control condition for women with binge-eating disorder to a 20-week DBT-based skills training group, they discovered that DBT patients showed more improvements in their binging, body image, eating concerns, and anger. While 86% of DBT participants reported no longer binging at the end of treatment, during the six-month follow-up, this percentage dropped to 56%. A second study contrasted a wait list condition with an altered version of individual DBT that included skills training. Binge and purging were less common in DBT patients. However, there is currently no follow-up data for this latter study.

Researchers compared the effects of an adapted version of DBT plus antidepressant medications versus medication alone in a study of elderly patients with depression who met criteria for a personality disorder. The results showed that at six months after treatment and post-treatment, a higher percentage of DBT patients had achieved depression remission.

In conclusion, parasuicidal women with BPD are among the patients for whom DBT has the strongest and most reliable empirical support. Promising evidence also exists regarding DBT for BPD-afflicted women who experience substance abuse issues. DBT may be helpful in lowering binge eating and other eating disorders, according to preliminary data. On the one hand, restricting DBT to women with BPD would be the most conservative clinical decision. For other clinical issues, however, DBT is a comprehensive approach that incorporates components of multiple evidence-based cognitive-behavioral interventions. Because of this, DBT is frequently used in clinical settings with multiproblematic patients in general, including those who have comorbid Axis I and II disorders, are suicidal, or engage in self-harm. Nevertheless, care should be taken when extending a treatment's use beyond the patients for whom it has been tested in research.

Crucial and Particular DBT Components

Some of the important and distinctive components of DBT are discussed in the section that follows. DBT is a thorough program that incorporates many elements of other cognitive-behavioral therapies, including cognitive restructuring, behavior therapy (including exposure, problem solving, contingency management, and stimulus control), and other similar interventions. The emphasis here is on those key components of treatment that are relatively specific and unique to DBT, such as:

(a) the five functions of treatment

(b) biosocial theory and emphasizing emotions in treatment

(c) dialectical philosophy

(d) acceptance and mindfulness, since many of these interventions are very similar to those found in other treatments.

Five purposes for the therapy. DBT is a comprehensive treatment program that includes group therapy, individual therapy, and a team of therapists for consultation. This makes DBT a treatment program as opposed to a single technique used by a practitioner on their own. Many times, clinicians are eager to use DBT but are intimidated by the thought of putting such a thorough treatment plan into practice. In this situation, it's crucial to keep in mind that the most crucial component of any DBT program is whether or not it covers the five essential treatment functions. While the most empirically supported DBT package is the standard version, there are situations where unique and inventive DBT applications are required. But in every situation, it's imperative that any DBT adaptation satisfies these five requirements:

Function #1: Increasing capacities. The underlying premise of DBT is that patients with BPD either lack or need to improve a number of critical life skills, such as the ability to:

(a) regulate emotions

(b) pay attention to the present moment and regulate attention

(c) navigate interpersonal situations effectively

(d) tolerate distress and survive crises without exacerbating the situation.

As a result, one of the main goals of DBT is skill improvement. Usually, four to ten people participate in a weekly skills group session that serves this purpose. The sessions include didactics, active practice, discussion of newly learned skills, and homework assignments to help patients continue practicing their skills in between sessions.

Function #2: Capabilities for generalization. It would be challenging to declare therapy successful if patients were unable to apply the skills they acquired in sessions to their everyday lives. Therefore, applying treatment successes to the patient's natural environment serves as a second crucial role of DBT. This task is completed in skill training by giving homework assignments for skill practice and troubleshooting advice on how to get better at practicing skills. Therapists assist patients in implementing new skills in their everyday lives during individual therapy sessions. They frequently ask patients to practice or apply new behaviors during these sessions. Furthermore, the patient can contact the therapist by phone in between sessions to receive assistance in applying skills during times of greatest need (e.g., in a crisis).

Function #3: Enhancing drive and decreasing maladaptive actions constitute. Enhancing patients' motivation to change and minimizing behaviors at odds with living a life worth living constitute a third role of DBT. The primary means of achieving this goal is through individual therapy. The patient fills out a self-monitoring form (also known as a "diary card") with the therapist once a week, tracking various treatment targets (such as self-harm, suicidal thoughts, and emotional distress). Using this diary card, the therapist assigns a higher priority to behaviors that endanger the patient's life (such as suicidal or self-injurious thoughts or actions), followed by behaviors that disrupt therapy (such as tardiness, absence, or non collaborative behavior), and behaviors that impair the patient's quality of life (such as severe living difficulties, unemployment, or severe issues associated with Axis I disorders).

The therapist works with the patient to identify the triggers for the behavior(s) in question as well as any potential aftereffects that could be sustaining the behavior(s) after prioritizing the behavioral targets for that particular session. In addition, the therapist assists the patient in discovering strategies for using effective, skillful behavior, resolving life's issues, or controlling emotions. Using a range of "commitment" techniques, the therapist actively attempts to get the patient to commit to changing their behavior in order to increase motivation.

Function #4: Enhancing and sustaining the motivation and abilities of the therapist. Keeping therapists who treat patients with BPD motivated and proficient is another crucial role of DBT. While working with multiproblematic BPD patients can be exciting and fulfilling, these patients also exhibit a strong range of behaviors that can strain the coping mechanisms, skills, and resolve of the professionals providing treatment (e.g., repeated suicidal thoughts, attempts at suicide, and behaviors that disrupt therapy). As a result, a system of offering therapists support, validation, ongoing education and skill development, feedback, and encouragement is a crucial component of an effective treatment plan for patients with BPD.

DBT therapists meet once a week for one to two hours to perform a therapist consultation-team meeting, which is a standard component of DBT. In order to implement effective treatment in the face of particular clinical challenges (such as a suicidal patient or a patient who misses sessions), the team works with therapists to solve problems. The team also monitors and assists in reducing therapist burnout, offers support and encouragement, and occasionally uses structured training or didactics on particular therapeutic skills. Finally, the team encourages therapists to maintain a compassionate, nonjudgmental orientation toward their patients.

Function #5: Setting up the surroundings. Restructuring the environment to promote progress and effective behavior while discouraging maladaptive or problematic behavior is a fourth key role of DBT. This frequently entails arranging the course of treatment in a way that best fosters advancement. In DBT, the primary therapist and person "in charge" of the treatment team is usually the individual therapist. He or she ensures that every component of a successful treatment plan is in place and that each of these requirements is fulfilled.

Assisting patients in rearranging their surroundings is another aspect of structuring the environment. For example, individuals who use drugs may need to learn how to change or stay away from social circles that encourage drug use; individuals who self-harm occasionally need to learn how to ensure that their partners or significant others do not encourage self-harm (i.e., by being unduly comforting, condescending, or supportive). In DBT, the therapist typically helps the patient change their surroundings, but occasionally, the therapist might actively help the patient make changes to their surroundings (for example, if the environment is too strong or overwhelming for the patient to have a reasonable degree of influence).

The biosocial theory and treatment approaches that prioritize feelings. Apart from fulfilling the aforementioned five purposes, DBT is founded on a theory of BPD that encourages practitioners to concentrate on emotions and emotion control during therapy. People with BPD are born with a temperament or disposition toward emotional vulnerability, according to the biosocial theory of BPD. A comparatively low threshold for reacting to emotional stimuli, strong emotional reactions, and trouble reverting to a baseline level of emotional arousal are the characteristics of emotional vulnerability. The child finds it difficult to learn coping mechanisms for such strong emotional reactions if parenting or child rearing is not done with extreme skill and effectiveness.

The primary environmental component is a parenting style that devalues the child's emotional reactions by rejecting, ridiculing, or punishing them or by oversimplifying how simple it is to cope with or solve problems. The child's propensity for emotional vulnerability interacts with the invalidating environment, raising the possibility of BPD. Because of this, the child lacks the ability to control their emotions, frequently experiences anxiety related to their emotions (also known as "emotion phobia"), and may turn to easily carried out, harmful coping mechanisms (such as intentional self-harm) as a means of managing their feelings.

DBT is an emotion-focused treatment that is based on the theory that BPD is a disorder of emotion dysregulation. DBT includes a number of behavioral skills that are specifically intended to teach patients how to recognize, understand, label, and regulate their emotions (i.e., the emotion regulation skills). This is because one of the main objectives of DBT is to improve patients' quality of life by reducing "…ineffective action tendencies associated with dysregulated emotions." Many of the most popular DBT interventions involve assisting patients in learning emotional regulation. The therapist addresses the patient's emotional reactions during sessions, especially when they impede progress.

Accordingly, therapists using DBT with BPD patients need to possess the abilities and know-how required to deal with emotions during treatment. A few more crucial skills for therapists are:

(a) recognizing emotions and their roles in problematic behavior.

(b) observing the patient's emotional reactions through changes in body language, voice tone, and other indicators of emotional states.

(c) assisting patients in accurately labeling emotional states

(d) validating emotional responses that are reasonable or that make sense given the circumstances.

(e) determining when specific skills are likely to be helpful in helping patients regulate (or accept) their emotions.

(d) instructing patients on how to use emotion regulation techniques when they are emotionally overwhelmed.

In DBT, dialectical philosophy. The primary factor that sets DBT apart from other cognitive-behavioral therapies is its dialectical philosophy. Although dialectical philosophy has been around for thousands of years in one form or another, it is most frequently connected to the ideas of Marx or Hegel. Within a dialectical framework, reality is made up of polar forces that are in conflict with each other. For example, patients' desire to be accepted rather than changed is increased when change-oriented treatment strategies are pushed for, which leads to tension. Additionally, dialectical philosophy asserts that opposing forces are constantly balanced and synthesized, and that none of them is complete on its own. In DBT, this is also the case. On the one hand, concentrating only on initiatives aimed at bringing about change was an insufficient approach because it was devoid of the necessary component of acceptance. However, concentrating only on accepting the patient can also be insufficient and ineffectual because suicidal, multiproblematic patients need significant life-altering interventions in order to live fulfilling lives.

The therapist's approach and style are influenced by dialectical thinking in many ways. For example, the therapist always aims to find the best way to combine and integrate acceptance and change-oriented techniques. The therapist strives to balance problem-solving and behavior-change techniques with acceptance and validation during each session. When recommending techniques or solutions, he or she frequently offers both change-based (solving the issue, altering behaviors, altering environments and reinforcement contingencies, altering cognitions) and acceptance-based (radical acceptance, tolerating discomfort, being aware of present emotional or other experiences) solutions. Dialectical thinking enables the therapist to let go of the need to be "right" and concentrate on finding ways to combine the patient's perspective and opinion with their own when they are at odds over a specific issue (based on the idea that each position is likely to be incomplete on its own). Lastly, DBT places a strong focus on flow, movement, and speed during therapy sessions. In addition to using a range of therapeutic techniques, therapists can be slow and methodical, reciprocal and validating, irreverent and off-beat, or vibrant and vivacious. Therapists also adjust their methods according to what is and is not effective at the time.

DBT emphasizes acceptance and mindfulness. Within Dialectical Behavior Therapy (DBT), a number of skills and interventions are designed to help the patient accept themselves, other people, and the world. One such remedy is practicing mindfulness. Mindfulness techniques aid patients in DBT by encouraging them to focus on the here and now. One way to practice mindfulness is to focus on effective, skillful behavior and attend to one thing at a time, or "one-mindfully," while also describing the facts of the current experience or situation, attending to and nonjudgmentally observing the current experience, and fully participating in the activity or experience of the present. In skills training, therapists instruct patients in mindfulness techniques, promote mindfulness in one-on-one counseling, and frequently engage in mindfulness practices themselves.

Another DBT acceptance intervention called radical acceptance is taught in the skills training module on distress tolerance. Radical acceptance is essentially accepting the experience of the present moment as it is, without resisting it or trying to change it. Conveying acceptance of the patient through validation, or confirming the truthfulness or validity of the patient's experience, feelings, ideas, or opinions, is the final acceptance intervention in DBT. Knowing when and how to apply the most effective acceptance-oriented strategies, given the patient's characteristics and difficulties as well as the therapy session's context, is a crucial skill for therapists practicing DBT, as was previously discussed.

To put it briefly, DBT is a comprehensive cognitive-behavioral therapy that was first created to assist women who were suicidal. The patient groups for which DBT has the greatest empirical support are parasuicidal women with BPD; however, patients with BPD and SUDs, individuals who fit the criteria for binge-eating disorder, and depressed elderly patients with personality disorders have also shown encouraging results. While DBT and other cognitive-behavioral approaches share many similarities, DBT treatment requires a few essential and distinctive components. Serving the five functions of treatment, the biosocial theory and emphasizing emotions in treatment, a consistent dialectical philosophy, mindfulness and acceptance-oriented interventions are a few of these components.

The Core Principles of DBT

The goal of dialectical behavior therapy (DBT), a cognitive-behavioral treatment, is to assist patients in acquiring efficient coping mechanisms, emotional control abilities, and interpersonal effectiveness. A set of fundamental ideas form the basis of DBT and direct its therapeutic methodology. This article explores these ideas in depth, offering a thorough grasp of the basic ideas that form the basis of DBT.

Dialectical Thinking

A key component of DBT is dialectical thinking, which stresses striking a balance between conflicting forces or viewpoints. This method recognizes that seemingly opposing viewpoints can coexist and be valid at the same time, and it encourages people to embrace both change and acceptance.

The fundamental tenet of dialectics is that everything is interrelated and subject to constant change. People can transcend inflexible, binary thought patterns—which frequently exacerbate emotional dysregulation and interpersonal challenges—by adopting this viewpoint. As an alternative, they can develop a more complex and adaptable understanding of their experiences, which will enable them to grow and change as individuals.

Therapists encourage their clients to experiment with different ways of thinking and acting while also supporting them in validating their feelings and experiences. Dialectical thinking is used in therapy by striking a balance between challenge and change and affirmation and support. This well-rounded strategy creates a setting where clients feel heard and inspired to make significant changes.

Mindfulness

Another fundamental tenet of DBT is mindfulness, which is developing a nonjudgmental, present-focused awareness of one's thoughts, feelings, and experiences. The goal of mindfulness practices is to provide a deeper connection between an individual's thoughts and emotions by assisting them in understanding their internal experiences.

By adding mindfulness into therapy, people can learn to recognize patterns and triggers that lead to emotional dysregulation and become more aware of their own emotional states. Having this knowledge is essential for creating practical coping mechanisms and enhancing emotional fortitude.

Additionally, mindfulness encourages self-acceptance and self-compassion, which lets people recognize their feelings without passing judgment. This nonjudgmental attitude can lessen the strength of unpleasant feelings and encourage a more balanced emotional reaction to trying circumstances.

Emotional Regulation

A key component of DBT is emotional regulation, which teaches people how to effectively control their emotions. This entails knowing how emotions work, identifying emotional cues, and creating coping mechanisms to lessen emotional sensitivity.

DBT provides a range of methods for managing emotions, such as cognitive restructuring, problem-solving, and self-soothing. By assisting people in better managing their emotions, these techniques lessen the possibility of impulsive or harmful behavior.

Furthermore, DBT's emotional regulation highlights how crucial it is to create positive experiences and develop resilience. Through participation in activities that foster happiness, contentment, and a feeling of achievement, people can fortify their emotional resilience and build a defense against adverse emotions.

Interpersonal Effectiveness

The last fundamental tenet of DBT is interpersonal effectiveness, which emphasizes enhancing interpersonal and communication abilities. The intention is to empower people to create more fulfilling and encouraging relationships by teaching them effective conflict resolution, boundary-setting, and need-assertion techniques.

DBT offers a range of methods and techniques to improve interpersonal effectiveness, including developing empathy, practicing assertiveness, and active listening. These abilities enable people to move through social situations with assurance and effectiveness, creating deeper relationships with others.

Through increasing interpersonal effectiveness, people can build a network of supportive people that is essential to their mental health and overall wellbeing. In difficult times, strong relationships can offer consolation, inspiration, and useful support, fostering resilience and general well-being.

To sum up, dialectical thinking, mindfulness, emotional regulation, and interpersonal effectiveness—the cornerstones of DBT—offer a thorough framework for assisting people in achieving emotional balance, creating meaningful relationships, and overcoming obstacles in life with resiliency. These ideas can help both therapists and clients use DBT to promote long-lasting transformation and personal development.

2

Chapter 2: The Four Modules of DBT

Mindfulness: Cultivating Present-Moment Awareness

Finding quiet moments in today's world of constant change and fast speed can be difficult. True contentment in the present moment is rare since our minds are so often consumed with regrets about the past or anxieties about the future. But mindfulness, a straightforward yet effective technique, provides us with a remedy for this restless mental state. We can open the door to a world of clarity, presence, and wellbeing by practicing mindfulness. This article delves into the fundamentals of mindfulness and examines how it can improve our physical, mental, and emotional health.

Knowing What Mindfulness Is

Fundamentally, mindfulness is the intentional, nonjudgmental practice of paying attention to the current moment. It entails purposefully focusing our attention on the feelings, ideas, and sensations that surface in every instant, avoiding becoming sucked into them or acting on an impulse. Although mindfulness has its roots in antiquated contemplative traditions like Buddhism, it has become increasingly popular as a secular practice that is open to people from all walks of life in recent years.

The Advantages of Being Present

1. Reducing Stress: By practicing mindfulness, we can learn to step back from the never-ending flow of ideas and concerns that cause stress. Stress levels can be lowered by making space for relaxation and introspection by objectively monitoring our thoughts and feelings.

2. Increasing Mental Clarity: Mindfulness training improves our capacity for concentration and focus. We can improve our creativity, decision-making abilities, and cognitive function by teaching our minds to be present. It has been demonstrated that mindfulness improves memory and attention span.

3. Improving Emotional Welfare: Being mindful encourages us to develop a kind and non-reactive connection with our feelings. We become more emotionally resilient and feel more in control of our responses when we acknowledge and accept our feelings. It lessens anxiety, depressive symptoms, and emotional reactivity.

4. Fostering Self-Awareness: Mindfulness promotes in-depth introspection and self-learning. We become more conscious of our routines, tendencies, and automatic reactions when we are totally present with ourselves. This increased self-awareness gives us the ability to choose wisely and stop engaging in harmful behaviors.

5. Promoting Physical Health: Studies indicate that mindfulness training can benefit one's physical well-being. Stress reduction strategies based on mindfulness have been associated with reduced blood pressure, better quality sleep, and a more robust immune system. Mindfulness can enhance general well-being by lowering stress and encouraging relaxation.

Including Mindfulness in Everyday Activities

1. Formal Practice of Meditation: Schedule a specific period of time every day to engage in mindfulness meditation. Locate a peaceful area, take a comfortable seat, and concentrate on your breathing or a particular feeling. As ideas come to mind, acknowledge them with kindness and then release them, bringing your attention back to the here and now. As you advance, gradually lengthen your sessions from shorter starts.

2. Mindful Activities: Incorporate mindfulness into routine tasks like walking, eating, and dishwashing. Take note of the taste, smell, texture, and movement as you engage with the senses. Feeling grounded and at ease can be attained by fully participating in these easy activities while maintaining present-moment awareness.

3. Mindful Breathing: Set aside some time to concentrate on your breathing whenever you're feeling anxious or overburdened. Shut your eyes, take a deep breath, then release it slowly, focusing only on the feeling of your breath entering and exiting your body. This easy exercise can help you regain your composure and focus your thoughts.

4. Non-Judgmental Observation: Make it a practice to observe your emotions, ideas, and physical experiences in a judgment-free manner. Observe experiences as they come and go rather than categorizing them as good or bad. This kind observation promotes acceptance and makes room for more comprehension and clarity.

By providing access to the richness and depth of the present moment, mindfulness helps us live more fully and truly. We can change the way we interact with the world and ourselves by adopting this practice. In a culture where distraction and busyness are the norm, mindfulness offers a useful tool for promoting holistic well-being, lowering stress levels, and achieving inner peace. Now, inhale deeply, enter the practice of mindfulness, and discover the many advantages of leading a life that is fully present.

Distress Tolerance: Coping with Crisis and Urges

Distress tolerance is a concept often associated with Dialectical Behavior Therapy (DBT), which was developed by Dr. Marsha Linehan. It refers to the ability to withstand and effectively manage emotional distress, particularly during crisis situations or when facing intense urges. Distress tolerance skills are crucial for individuals who may struggle with overwhelming emotions, impulsive behaviors, or difficulty managing crisis situations.

Here are some distress tolerance skills commonly taught in DBT:

1.Self-Soothing: Engaging in activities that provide comfort and a sense of calm. This might include taking a warm bath, listening to soothing music, or engaging in activities that bring a sense of peace.

2.Distract with ACCEPTS: This acronym represents a set of distraction techniques:

- Activities: Engage in activities that require concentration.
- Contributing: Help others or engage in acts of kindness.
- Comparisons: Compare your current situation to a worse one you have experienced or imagined.
- Emotions: Generate different emotions by engaging in activities that create a specific mood.
- Pushing Away: Mentally set aside the issue for a specific period.
- Thoughts: Focus your mind on something else.

3.Self-Soothe with the 5 Senses: Use your five senses to engage in activities that provide comfort. This might involve looking at beautiful scenery, listening to calming music, smelling pleasant scents, tasting something enjoyable, or feeling the texture of a comforting object.

4.Pros and Cons List: Weigh the pros and cons of engaging in a particular behavior. This helps individuals make more informed decisions rather than acting impulsively.

5.Radical Acceptance: Acknowledge and accept the reality of a situation, even if it's unpleasant. This can help reduce emotional suffering and allow for more effective problem-solving.

6.Turning the Mind: Make a conscious decision to accept and tolerate the current situation rather than fighting against it. This involves choosing to participate in the moment rather than resisting.

7.Wise Mind:

- Reasonable Mind: Making decisions based on facts and logic.
- Emotion Mind: Making decisions based on emotions and feelings.
- Wise Mind: Combining both reason and emotion to make balanced and effective decisions.

8.Improve the Moment: Engage in activities that are enjoyable or provide a sense of accomplishment to improve your mood and help cope with distress.

It's important to note that distress tolerance skills are just one component of DBT. DBT also includes mindfulness, interpersonal effectiveness, and emotion regulation skills. Individuals are encouraged to practice these skills regularly, not just during moments of crisis, to enhance their ability to cope with distressing situations over time. If you or someone you know is struggling with distress or urges, it's advisable to seek professional help from a mental health professional or therapist.

Emotion Regulation: Managing Intense Feelings

Feelings are a natural aspect of daily existence. When we are caught in traffic, we become irritated. When we miss our loved ones, we get depressed. When someone disappoints us or injures us, we may become enraged.

Even though we anticipate experiencing these feelings frequently, some people begin to feel more erratic emotions. Their lives start to be affected by these peaks and valleys as they experience greater highs and lower lows. People with strong emotional swings can be serene one minute and depressed or furious the next.

Although everyone experiences moments when their emotions spiral out of control, some people experience this on a regular basis. They may say and do things they later regret as a result of their quickly shifting emotions. They might jeopardize their credibility or sour relationships.

A person may become emotionally uncontrollable for a variety of reasons. They might be more susceptible to these quick changes due to genetics. They might not have learned the skills or seen positive models of emotional regulation. When they come across events that remind them of unpleasant experiences from the past, they might lose control. Physical changes like fatigue or a drop in blood sugar can also make someone lose control of their emotions.

Whatever the cause of our emotional instability, we can improve our self-regulation skills, which is good news. Learning how to manage our emotions is something that can help all of us. The capacity to more effectively manage our emotions is known as emotional regulation.

What do emotional regulation and control mean?

Any action that modifies the intensity of an emotional experience falls under the category of emotional control and regulation. It does not imply repressing or evading feelings. You have control over the emotions you experience and the way you express them when you have emotional regulation skills.

In the end, it all comes down to having the capacity to successfully regulate our emotions using a variety of strategies.

A person's ability to control their emotions varies from person to person. They have a high emotional intelligence and are conscious of their own emotions as well as those of others. Despite the impression that they are simply "naturally calm," these people also feel bad sometimes. They've only recently acquired coping mechanisms that let them control challenging emotions.

Fortunately, emotional self-regulation is a dynamic quality. It is possible to acquire and develop emotional regulation abilities over time. Your physical and mental well-being can both benefit from learning how to cope with unpleasant events.

Why is emotional control crucial?

It is expected of us as adults to control our emotions in a way that both benefits society and allows us to get by in life. Problems can arise when our emotions take control of us.

Emotional regulation can be hampered by numerous things. These include our perceptions of unpleasant feelings or our inability to control our emotions. Stressful circumstances can occasionally elicit particularly strong feelings.

The effect emotional instability can have on our interpersonal relationships is one way it can harm us. For instance, we are prone to say hurtful things to people around us and make them distance themselves when we are unable to control our anger. We might have to spend time mending relationships or regret the things we've said.

Not only can an inability to control our emotions harm our relationships, but it can also cause us harm personally. Overwhelming melancholy can diminish wellbeing and result in needless suffering. Unrelenting fear can prevent us from taking chances and experiencing new things in life.

5 techniques you should learn to control your emotions

We can learn a variety of techniques to control our emotions.

1. Make room.
Emotions come on quickly. Instead of thinking, "Now I will be angry," we just get tight-lipped and enraged all of a sudden. So pausing is the best gift we can give ourselves when it comes to managing challenging emotions. Inhaled deeply. Reduce the speed at which the trigger and response occur.

2. Being aware of your feelings
Being able to recognize your feelings is a skill that is just as vital. The practices that Dr. Judson Brewer, MD, Ph.D. suggests can help you become more inquisitive about your own bodily reactions. Pay attention to yourself and ask yourself, where in your body are you feeling things? Are you feeling nauseous? Is your pulse pounding? Do you have a headache or neck tension?

Your physical symptoms may be indicators of your emotional state. Asking questions about your physical state can also divert your attention and lessen the intensity of the feeling.

3. Labeling your emotions
The ability to name your feelings can help you regain control over your

circumstances after you've noticed them. What term would you use to describe the feelings you are experiencing? Is it resentment, sadness, anger, or disappointment? What is it, again? Fear is one powerful feeling that frequently lurks beneath others.

It's common for us to experience multiple emotions simultaneously, so don't be afraid to name any feelings you may be experiencing. Next, delve a little further. What are you afraid of, if you are afraid? If you're angry, what or whom are you angry with? Gaining the ability to identify your feelings will bring you one step closer to expressing them to other people.

4. Embracing the feeling

It is normal and natural for us to react to situations with emotions. Acknowledge that your feelings of anger or fear are legitimate rather than punishing yourself for them. Make an effort to be kind to yourself and extend grace to yourself. Acknowledge that feeling emotions is a typical human response.

5. Making mindfulness a habit

Being mindful involves being aware of our inner selves, which enables us to "live in the moment." Make nonjudgmental observations about what is going on around you by using your senses. These abilities can assist you in maintaining composure and preventing destructive thought patterns when experiencing emotional distress.

Seven techniques to help you control your emotions

People can develop a variety of emotion regulation techniques to strengthen their coping mechanisms. It's critical to evaluate which tactics are most effective and which ones to steer clear of.

Two major categories can be used to describe emotional regulation. The first is reappraisal, which involves altering our perspective on a situation in order to modify our reaction. Suppression is the second, and it is associated with more unfavorable results. Studies reveal that suppressing our feelings is linked to unhappiness and low wellbeing.

Let's examine seven techniques for constructive and healthful emotion management.

1. Determine and lessen stressors

It is not advisable to try to suppress or be afraid of negative feelings. However, you also don't have to continuously place yourself in uncomfortable situations. When you begin to experience strong emotions, start observing any patterns or contributing factors. Honesty and curiosity are needed for this. Did you experience a sense of smallness? Strong feelings, especially the ones we keep hidden, frequently arise from our ingrained fears. What is going on in your immediate surroundings, and what memories does it trigger for you?

Once you've determined which triggers they are, you can investigate why they are so important and whether you can lessen their influence. For example, a CEO who struggled in math class might be embarrassed to admit that he gets angry when talking about numbers. Maybe knowing this trigger is sufficient. Alternatively, the CEO may decide to see a private preview of the monthly charts in order to prevent feeling as though he is being delayed by everyone else.

2. Pay attention to bodily complaints

Be mindful of your emotions, particularly whether you are feeling fatigued or hungry. These elements may intensify your feelings and lead you to interpret them more strongly. You can alter your emotional reaction if you can take care of the underlying problem (such as hunger or tiredness).

3. Think about the narrative you are telling yourself.

When information is lacking, we provide our own details to fill in the gaps. If you haven't heard from a family member in a while, you might be feeling rejected and thinking they don't care about you anymore.

Consider your options before assigning blame. What other explanations might exist? What else might be going on with the family member in the example that would prevent them from contacting you? Might they be ill or preoccupied? Do they have good intentions but a habit of forgetting to keep their word?

Add "just like me" at the end, regardless of the other person's motivation or course of action (there is almost always another person involved). It serves as a helpful reminder that they are also fallible human beings.

4. Use constructive self-talk

We may start telling ourselves things like, "I messed up again," or "everyone else is so awful," when our emotions get too much for us to handle. Positive comments can take the place of some of this negative self-talk if you treat yourself with empathy. Sayings like "I always try so hard" or "People are doing the best they can" can help you feel better about yourself. This change may lessen the intensity of our feelings. You no longer have to place blame or extrapolate the problem beyond the context in order to express your frustration with a situation that isn't working.

5. Select your course of action.

Most of the time, we can choose our course of action. You probably realize how your relationships are suffering if you frequently react to angry feelings by snapping at people. It's possible that you'll also notice that it hurts. Alternatively, even though it feels good right now, the long-term effects hurt.

Remember that you have the power to decide how you want to react the next time you experience fear or anger. That acknowledgment has great power.

Maybe you should try responding differently instead of lash out? Is it possible for you to express your anger to someone without using harsh language? Become inquisitive about the outcomes of altering your answers. What was your feeling? What was the other person's reaction?

6. Seek out happy feelings

It is in our nature to give negative emotions greater weight than positive ones. We call this negativity bias. Emotions that are negative, such as disgust, anger, and sadness, often have a high emotional weight. Contentment, curiosity, and thankfulness are quieter emotions. Developing the practice of recognizing these good things can increase resilience and general wellbeing.

7. Look for a counselor

Controlling our own feelings is not always easy. A high level of self-awareness is necessary. We start to lose our ability to control our emotions when we're going through a difficult period. We occasionally require a partner, such as a therapist, to assist us in developing stronger self-regulation abilities. Thankfully, there are lots of therapeutic approaches that can teach us how to control our emotions more effectively.

Emotional regulation disorder: what is it?

A person with emotional regulation disorder struggles to control their emotions. Dysregulation is the term used to describe this inadequate emotional regulation. The inability to control one's emotions or maintain reactions within a reasonable bound is known as dysregulation.

Dramatic mood swings are more likely to occur in someone with emotional regulation disorder. These variations then have a detrimental effect on the individual's behavior.

A disorder of emotional regulation may cause some of the following symptoms:

- Having trouble establishing and preserving healthy relationships
- Acts of self-destruction
- Excessive sensitivity
- Frequently having tantrums or meltdowns

Emotional outbursts directed at someone who did not cause the harm

Other mental health conditions may coexist with emotional regulation disorder. Emotional regulation is frequently made more difficult by disorders like borderline personality disorder, depression, or stress.

Interpersonal Effectiveness: Building Healthy Relationships

The establishment and upkeep of healthy relationships is the aim of DBT's interpersonal effectiveness skills. Those who have lived long, fulfilling lives in healthy relationships frequently possess these abilities naturally. These qualities have been broken down by DBT and transformed into four distinct skills. Everyone can benefit from learning these techniques, but those who suffer from attachment disorders or have experienced trauma will benefit most.

THINK

The more recent DBT interpersonal effectiveness skill is THINK. It was created to lessen animosity toward other people. Although you won't always need to use this skill, it will come in handy when you're having trouble with others and you're feeling down.

Consider the circumstances from the viewpoint of the other person. Is she also furious? Do you think you're unreasonable, and she thinks you're unreasonable?

Demonstrate empathy by asking yourself how the other person might feel. Give yourself a moment to experience her feelings.

Interpretations: of the actions of the other person. Consider potential explanations for her actions that offended you. To help you stay open-minded, start with ludicrous justifications before moving on to more sensible ones.

"She works for the lab and is doing tests on how mean she can be and get away with it. She wasn't raised in the lab, but she was raised in a lab and doesn't have a heart. Her hamster passed away this morning, and she's using meanness to hide her grief → She battles depression and recently had a meltdown that led to her being unpleasant. As a human, she became irritated and didn't handle it well. Everybody makes errors.

Hopefully, after completing these first three steps, you will feel less angry and be able to think and act more rationally. That will assist you in the next two steps.

Observe the other individual: Observe her attempts to be considerate and enhance the bond between them. Even though you assumed she was angry, you can see that she appears afraid. Even though you may not be friends just yet, you should have noticed that she smiled at you. Just take note of it; there's nothing you need to do about it right now.

Generosity in your answer: This does not require you to forget and forgive right away. This merely indicates that you speak with kindness. "I hope we can fix this in the future. What you said to me hurt." might be your response. I need some space right now. In the long run, a polite reply will be more beneficial to the relationship than shouting and name-calling.

One could classify the acronym THINK as an interpersonal distress tolerance skill. The following interpersonal effectiveness techniques will be easy for you to apply once you're in a position where you feel capable of controlling your feelings toward the other individual.

FAST

FAST focuses on preserving your dignity in the face of disagreement. Prior to using them all at once, you should use them sequentially.

Fair: Both to others and to yourself. This encompasses your ideas as well as your behavior. "I'm powerless in this situation" or "They're the worst!" are examples of dramatic or judgmental thoughts or statements that you do not use when you are being fair. As an alternative, you might be thinking something like, "What's going on for that person, and what's going on for me?" or "What were the elements of truth, even though I didn't agree with most of what he just said?"

No: Sorry doesn't mean you should never apologize; in fact, apologizing has a tremendously positive effect on relationships. But when you haven't done anything wrong, you don't have to apologize.

Maintain your morals: Take a stance for your beliefs. If you're unsure of your beliefs, examine yourself to find out what your values are. Tell the truth about your values. You cannot truly value family if you claim to value them but actively avoid them. You might want to jot down your current values as well as your ideal values for the future.

Sincere: Be sincere with both yourself and other people. Are you making things worse than they are? Do you downplay it? Are you being honest?

Regardless of how you feel about the result, you can keep your composure and leave a situation feeling good about yourself by following the four steps of FAST.

Though they can be applied to all forms of interpersonal communication, THINK and FAST are particularly useful in conflictual situations. You can develop a good relationship through regular interpersonal communication by using the techniques GIVE and DEAR MAN.

GIVE

In any kind of interpersonal interaction, the GIVE skill is beneficial. Regardless of the length of time you've been married or met this person, GIVE will support the development and upkeep of healthy relationships.

Gentle in your manner: Being gentle means that you are considerate of the feelings of the other person. By doing this, you can make the other person feel more loved and less attacked during your conversation. When there is no defensiveness, communication is always more effective.

Curious about what the other person has to say: Expressions of interest can be expressed verbally or nonverbally. You can use words to probe the person with inquiries about her statements or to elicit simple "huh" or "oh really?" reactions. Making a facial expression, keeping eye contact, and paying attention to what is being said are all ways to show interest through body language.

Validate: By reflecting back to the other person the feelings you are experiencing, you can demonstrate to her that you have heard and understood what she is saying. You might respond, "How frustrating! "if she tells you that her friend has canceled their lunch date for the third time in a row. You have to be really disappointed!

Easy manner: Throughout the conversation, project a sense of ease and comfort. You'll come across as more friendly.

For the GIVE skill to be used, communication must be both verbal and nonverbal. You'll be better equipped to communicate with people in all of your relationships if you take these steps.

DEAR MAN

The interpersonal skill known as "DEAR MAN" is the ability to politely and effectively make requests in order to establish and preserve a relationship, regardless of whether you end up getting what you want.

Give a brief description of the circumstances: Saying something like "My friends are going to see the new comic book movie this weekend" can succinctly sum up your plans to go to the movies with your pals.

Tell people what you want: "I'd like to accompany them to the movies."
In a polite, non-aggressive manner, state why this is important to you. "It would be really meaningful if I could spend time with them because I haven't been able to since the track season started."

When you do receive what you requested, reinforce: "I swear, before I head out to the movie, my room will be spotless and my homework completed."
Be mindful and remain in the present. Don't stress about the past or the future, or about what people will think of you if you are unable to attend. Simply stay in that instant.

Look Assured: Are you incredibly afraid to ask your boss for a raise? That's not necessary for her to know. Be sure to approach the matter with assurance.

When it doesn't seem like you're going to get the outcome you were hoping for, negotiate and show some flexibility. Find a mutually agreeable middle ground by negotiating.

Many teenagers make demands, ask incoherently, or don't ask at all in favor of getting what they want instead of asking for what they need.
Not only can interpersonal effectiveness skills benefit individuals dealing with attachment disorders and borderline personality disorder, but they can also benefit anyone looking to improve their relationships with others.

3

Chapter 3: Skills Training and Practical Exercises

Learning and Applying Mindfulness Techniques

Mindfulness is a practice that involves bringing one's attention to the present moment. It has its roots in ancient contemplative traditions, particularly in Buddhism, but in recent years, it has gained widespread popularity as a secular practice with numerous mental and physical health benefits. Learning and applying mindfulness techniques can be transformative for individuals in managing stress, improving focus, and enhancing overall well-being.

Learning Mindfulness Techniques:

Start with the Basics:

Begin with simple mindfulness exercises. Focus on your breath, sensations in your body, or the sounds around you.

Mindful breathing is a common starting point. Pay attention to your breath, the rise and fall of your chest or the sensation of air passing through your nostrils.

Guided Meditations:

Use guided meditations led by experienced instructors. Many resources, including apps and online platforms, offer guided sessions to help beginners establish a routine.

Mindful Observation:

Engage in mindful observation of your surroundings. Take notice of colors, shapes, and details. This helps anchor your awareness in the present moment.

Body Scan:

Practice a body scan meditation, where you systematically bring attention to each part of your body. This helps in developing body awareness and relaxation.

Non-judgmental Awareness:

Cultivate non-judgmental awareness of your thoughts and feelings. Instead of labeling them as good or bad, simply observe and acknowledge them without attachment.

Applying Mindfulness Techniques:
In Daily Activities:

Bring mindfulness into daily routines. Whether it's eating, walking, or washing dishes, focus on the activity at hand instead of letting your mind wander.

Mindful Breathing in Stressful Situations:

When faced with stress, practice mindful breathing. Take a few deep breaths, focusing on each inhale and exhale. This can help regulate emotions and reduce the impact of stressors.

Mindful Listening:

Practice mindful listening in conversations. Truly pay attention to what others are saying without mentally preparing your response. This improves communication and empathy.

Mindful Work:
Apply mindfulness at work. Take short breaks to focus on your breath or engage in brief mindfulness exercises to enhance concentration and reduce workplace stress.

Mindful Walking:
Incorporate mindful walking into your routine. Pay attention to the sensation of each step, the movement of your body, and the environment around you.

Mindfulness Apps:
Use mindfulness apps that offer reminders and guided sessions. These can help you integrate mindfulness into your daily life and provide support in developing a consistent practice.

Challenges and Tips:
Consistency is Key:
Like any skill, mindfulness requires consistent practice. Set aside dedicated time each day for your mindfulness practice.

Patience and Non-Judgment:
Be patient with yourself. It's natural for the mind to wander. When it happens, gently bring your focus back to the present without judgment.

Adapt to Preferences:
Explore different mindfulness techniques and find what works best for you. Some people may prefer sitting meditation, while others find mindfulness in movement (e.g., yoga) more effective.

Community Support:
Joining a mindfulness group or community can provide support and

motivation. Sharing experiences and insights with others can enhance your mindfulness journey.

Incorporating mindfulness into your life is a personal and ongoing process. It's not about achieving a particular state but rather about cultivating awareness and presence in each moment. As you continue to practice, you may find that mindfulness becomes a valuable tool for managing stress, improving focus, and fostering overall well-being.

Developing Distress Tolerance Strategies

The ability to tolerate discomfort is essential for handling difficult and upsetting circumstances. People can better manage stress, hardship, and emotional discomfort by learning how to tolerate discomfort. These techniques are frequently a mainstay of dialectical behavior therapy (DBT), a therapeutic modality that places a strong emphasis on developing emotional regulation skills. The following are some crucial elements and methods for increasing distress tolerance:

Comprehending Distress Tolerance
Acknowledging Reality:
Recognize and come to terms with the fact that suffering exists. Denying or avoiding upsetting circumstances can frequently make the issue worse. The first step toward effective distress tolerance is acceptance.

Crisis versus distress:
Differentiate between a crisis and distress. Distress is not always comfortable, but a crisis calls for quick response. Making the right coping strategy decisions is aided by understanding the differences.
Techniques for Tolerating Distress:

Being mindful:

To maintain your sense of present-moment awareness, engage in mindfulness. To build a mental space that can withstand discomfort, try practicing mindful breathing and nonjudgmental thought observation.

Self-Relieving Tasks:

Take part in relaxing and comfortable activities. This can entail spending time in nature, having a warm bath, or listening to relaxing music.

Strategies for Diversion:

Turn your attention away from upsetting ideas or circumstances for a short while. To take a mental vacation, this could entail reading a book, watching a movie, or taking up a hobby.

Skills to Survive a Crisis:

Learn specialized crisis management techniques, such as assembling a crisis survival kit with items and activities that offer solace and diversion.

Wise mind:

Develop the ability to access your "wise mind," which is a mind that balances reason and emotion. This entails using both reason and emotion to inform decisions.

TIPP Skills:

Quickly lowering emotional arousal can be achieved by using techniques like temperature, intense exercise, paced breathing, and paired muscle relaxation (TIPP). Doing vigorous exercise or sprinkling cold water on your face, for instance, can instantly calm you down.

Radical Acknowledgment:

Accept with radicalism that there are things in life that are out of your control. Although it doesn't mean you have to agree with the circumstances, accepting them can lessen emotional pain.

List of Pros and Cons:

Make a list of the benefits and drawbacks of giving in to your impulses. This aids in weighing the possible outcomes and enabling more informed decision-making.

Gratitude in Self-Talk:

Use self-talk that is uplifting and affirming to combat negative thoughts. Swap out catastrophic thinking for more realistic and balanced viewpoints.

Advice for Acquiring a Distress-Tolerance

Continual Application:

Distress tolerance gets better with practice, just like any other skill. Even when there isn't a crisis, practice distress tolerance exercises on a regular basis to strengthen the abilities.

Create a Toolbox:

Assemble a toolkit containing different approaches to handle stress. Not every tactic is effective in every circumstance, so flexibility is made possible by having a range of tools.

Consult a Professional:

If you're struggling to create and apply distress tolerance techniques on your own, think about getting help from a mental health professional.

Think and Grow:

After applying techniques for distress tolerance, consider what went well and what didn't. By reflecting on yourself, you can improve how you handle situations in the future.

Include Others Who Can Help:

Talk about your goals for distress tolerance with friends or family who will be encouraging. Support networks can offer accountability and motivation.

Recall that everyone's journey is different and that distress tolerance is a skill that can be developed over time.

You can strengthen your resilience and improve your capacity to handle difficult situations by adopting these techniques into your everyday life and regularly using them. If you're having trouble putting these strategies into practice on your own, consulting a mental health professional can offer you individualized support and help.

Mastering Emotion Regulation Skills

Maintaining mental health and controlling one's emotional reactions to different circumstances require the ability to regulate emotions. Acquiring these abilities entails comprehending, embracing, and regulating feelings in a manner that fosters flexible conduct and mental well-being. The following are essential elements and techniques for developing emotion regulation skills:

Comprehending Emotion Management

Emotional Consciousness:

Accurately recognize and label the emotions you are experiencing. Effective emotion regulation is built on this self-awareness.

Distinguishing Between Emotions:

Acknowledge the subtle distinctions among different feelings. Knowing whether you're experiencing joy, sadness, anxiety, or anger enables you to use more focused regulation techniques.

The Mind-Body Link:

Keep an eye out for the bodily manifestations of various emotions. Comprehending the physiological expression of emotions can furnish supplementary indications for self-regulation.

Strategies for Regulating Emotions

Cognitive Evaluation:

Modify your perspective on a situation to affect your emotional reaction. This entails rephrasing ideas to produce a more optimistic or balanced viewpoint.

Acceptance and Mindfulness:

By being mindful, you can observe and accept your feelings without passing judgment. This entails living in the present and letting feelings come and go without letting them control you.

Techniques for Deep Breathing and Relaxation:

Practice progressive muscle relaxation and deep breathing techniques to soothe your body's physiological reaction to stress and intense emotions.

Write with Expression:

Processing and regulating your emotions can be aided by keeping a journal of your feelings and experiences. Write about your feelings, examining the underlying ideas and beliefs, along with the reasons behind them.

Activation of Behavior:

Take part in things that make you feel happy or accomplished. Emotions and mood can benefit from positive behaviors.

Effectiveness of Interactions:

Learn how to communicate effectively so that you can assertively express your needs and emotions. Emotional distress can be decreased and misunderstandings can be avoided with clear communication.

Establish a Secure Area:

Choose a place, either mental or physical, where you can go when you're feeling overwhelmed. This could be a peaceful room, a well-liked outdoor location, or just a safety-inducing visualization exercise.

Establish Limits:

Healthy boundaries should be established and communicated in your relationships. By being aware of and open about your boundaries, you can avoid emotional overload.

Ask for Social Assistance:

Discuss your feelings with a therapist, family member, or trusted friend. Social support can offer perspective, empathy, and validation.

Suggestions for Developing Emotional Control

Exercise Frequently:

Practice makes perfect when it comes to the skill of emotion regulation. Participate in routine exercises and techniques to strengthen and bolster your skills.

Consider the Patterns:

Consider any recurrent themes in your emotional reactions. Targeted intervention is possible when triggers and typical reactions are understood.

Create a Toolbox:

Create a customized toolkit with the tactics that are most effective for you. Being adaptable in various circumstances is made possible by having a diverse set of tools.

Self-Restraint:

Have empathy for yourself. Recognize that a variety of emotions are felt by everyone and that it's acceptable to do so. You should be kind to yourself as you would a friend.

Take Advice from Experience

After resolving difficult emotional situations, consider what went well and what didn't. Make use of these observations to improve your strategy going forward.

Consult a Professional:

Seeking the advice of a mental health professional is something you should think about if you're having trouble learning how to control your emotions. They are able to offer tailored advice and tactics.

Being able to control your emotions is a continuous process that requires practice, self-awareness, and a dedication to personal development. Through the daily application of these strategies and consistent practice, you can improve your capacity for effective emotion regulation, which will improve your mental and emotional health.

Enhancing Interpersonal Effectiveness

Enhancing interpersonal effectiveness involves developing and refining skills that contribute to positive and productive interactions with others. Effective interpersonal skills are crucial for building healthy relationships, both personally and professionally. Here are key aspects and strategies for enhancing interpersonal effectiveness:

Key Components of Interpersonal Effectiveness

Communication Skills:

Develop clear and assertive communication. Express your thoughts, feelings, and needs openly while respecting the perspectives of others.

Practice active listening to fully understand what others are communicating. This involves giving your full attention, asking clarifying questions, and paraphrasing to ensure understanding.

Empathy:

Cultivate empathy by putting yourself in others' shoes. Understand and validate their feelings and perspectives, even if you don't agree. Empathy fosters connection and mutual understanding.

Conflict Resolution:

Learn effective conflict resolution skills. Address conflicts calmly and constructively, focusing on finding solutions rather than placing blame.

Use "I" statements to express how you feel and what you need, which can help reduce defensiveness in others.

Setting Boundaries:

Establish and communicate clear boundaries in your relationships. This involves knowing your limits and expressing them assertively to maintain a healthy balance.

Non-Verbal Communication:

Be mindful of your body language, facial expressions, and gestures. Non-verbal cues can convey as much, if not more, information than words.

Adaptability:

Be flexible and adaptable in your communication style. Adjust your approach based on the needs and preferences of the individuals or groups you are interacting with.

Social Awareness:

Develop social awareness by being attuned to social cues and dynamics. Understand the emotional tone of a situation and adjust your behavior accordingly.

Interpersonal Effectiveness Strategies:

DEARMAN:

Use the DEARMAN acronym (Describe, Express, Assert, Reinforce, Stay Mindful, Appear Confident) from Dialectical Behavior Therapy (DBT) to effectively assert yourself in interpersonal situations.

GIVE:

Employ the GIVE acronym (Gentle, Interested, Validate, Easy Manner) to enhance your ability to be assertive while maintaining positive relationships.

Clarify Expectations:

Clearly communicate expectations in relationships and collaborative efforts. This includes expressing your expectations and understanding the expectations of others.

Positive Feedback:

Provide positive and constructive feedback. Acknowledge others for their strengths and contributions, and offer feedback in a way that promotes growth and improvement.

Apologize Effectively:

Learn to apologize sincerely and take responsibility for your actions. A genuine apology involves acknowledging the impact of your behavior and expressing a commitment to positive change.

Cultural Sensitivity:

Be culturally sensitive and aware of diversity in your interactions. Respect and appreciate differences in cultural backgrounds, perspectives, and communication styles.

Tips for Enhancing Interpersonal Effectiveness:

Self-Reflection: Regularly reflect on your interpersonal interactions. Consider what went well and areas for improvement. Self-awareness is the foundation for growth.

Continuous Learning: Be open to learning and improving your interpersonal skills continuously. Seek feedback from others and actively work on addressing areas of challenge.

Build Rapport: Invest time in building positive relationships. Foster rapport by showing genuine interest in others, remembering details about them, and being reliable and trustworthy.

Conflict Prevention: Proactively address potential sources of conflict. Open communication and addressing issues early can prevent conflicts from escalating.

Seek Professional Development: Consider professional development opportunities, such as workshops or courses on communication and interpersonal skills. This can provide structured learning and practical strategies.

Model Effective Behavior: Demonstrate the interpersonal skills you value in others. Modeling positive behavior can influence the dynamics of your relationships and encourage others to respond in kind.

Enhancing interpersonal effectiveness is an ongoing process that requires self-awareness, practice, and a commitment to building positive connections with others. By incorporating these strategies into your daily interactions and consistently working on developing your skills, you can strengthen your interpersonal effectiveness and contribute to healthier and more fulfilling relationships.

4

Chapter 4: The Role of Dialectics in DBT

Understanding Dialectical Thinking

In DBT, the term "dialectical" refers to the synthesis of opposites. Here are some key aspects of understanding dialectical thinking in DBT:

Synthesis of Opposites: Dialectical Thinking involves accepting and integrating opposing viewpoints or apparent contradictions. It encourages individuals to recognize the validity of different perspectives and find a middle ground.

Dialectical Dilemmas: Individuals often experience internal conflicts or dilemmas. These are situations where two seemingly opposite things can both be true. For example, a person might feel both the need for independence and the desire for connection. DBT helps individuals navigate these dilemmas and find a balance.

Validation and Change:DBT emphasizes the importance of validating a person's experience while also encouraging change. Validating means acknowledging and accepting the individual's feelings and thoughts, even if they seem contradictory. At the same time, the therapy promotes change by helping individuals develop skills to manage their emotions and behaviors effectively.

Acceptance and Commitment: Dialectical Thinking includes the concept of radical acceptance. This involves fully accepting the current situation, even if it's painful or difficult, while also recognizing the need for change. The goal is to find a balance between acceptance and commitment to personal growth and positive change.

Dialectical Behavior Therapy (DBT) Skills: DBT includes specific skills training modules, and these skills are designed to help individuals develop a more dialectical approach to thinking and behaving. For example, distress tolerance skills help individuals cope with difficult emotions, while emotion regulation skills focus on understanding and managing intense emotions.

Balancing Caring for Self and Others: Dialectical Thinking in DBT encourages individuals to find a balance between caring for themselves and considering the needs of others. This is important for building and maintaining healthy relationships.

Nonjudgmental Stance: Practicing a nonjudgmental stance is crucial in DBT. It involves approaching thoughts, feelings, and behaviors without harsh judgment. This nonjudgmental perspective fosters a more open and receptive mindset.

By incorporating dialectical thinking, DBT aims to help individuals overcome rigid, black-and-white thinking patterns, reduce impulsive behaviors, and develop more adaptive ways of managing emotions and interpersonal challenges. It is particularly effective for individuals struggling with emotion dysregulation, self-harm, and relationship difficulties.

Balancing Acceptance and Change

The approach emphasizes finding a synthesis between accepting the present reality and committing to making positive changes. Here's an exploration of how this balance is achieved:

Dialectical Abstinence: DBT encourages a balance between accepting where a person is at the moment and committing to change. This is often referred to as "dialectical abstinence." It means that even as individuals work towards changing harmful behaviors, they accept that, in the short term, complete abstinence may be challenging. This acceptance can reduce the shame and guilt associated with setbacks, fostering a more compassionate and realistic mindset.

Radical Acceptance: A key concept in DBT is radical acceptance, which involves fully acknowledging and embracing the reality of the current situation without judgment. It doesn't mean approving or liking the situation; rather, it's about accepting what is. This acceptance is a necessary foundation for change, as it allows individuals to move forward without being weighed down by resistance or denial.

Validation: Validation is an essential aspect of DBT. Therapists work to validate the individual's feelings, thoughts, and experiences, reinforcing the idea that their reactions are understandable given their unique circumstances. Validating emotions creates an environment of understanding and acceptance, promoting a sense of self-worth.

Behavioral Change Strategies: While accepting the current state is important, DBT is also action-oriented. It provides specific behavioral change strategies to help individuals develop healthier coping mechanisms, improve emotional regulation, and enhance interpersonal skills. This commitment to change is integral to the therapeutic process.

Mindfulness: Mindfulness is a core component of DBT and plays a crucial role in balancing acceptance and change. Mindfulness involves paying attention to the present moment without judgment. By cultivating mindfulness, individuals can observe their thoughts and emotions without getting entangled in them, promoting both acceptance and change.

Dialectical Strategies: Therapists in DBT often use dialectical strategies to help individuals navigate seemingly conflicting goals. For example, finding a balance between accepting oneself as they are while also acknowledging the need for personal growth. These strategies promote flexibility in thinking and behavior.

Commitment to Therapy: Engaging in DBT requires a commitment to the therapeutic process. This commitment involves both accepting the challenges of the present and actively working towards change. The therapeutic relationship itself embodies the dialectic of acceptance and change, providing a supportive and validating environment for growth.

The balance between acceptance and change in DBT is not a static state but a dynamic process. Individuals move through stages of acceptance and commitment, gradually building a more resilient and skillful approach to life's challenges. This synthesis of acceptance and change is at the heart of DBT's effectiveness in helping individuals create a life worth living.

5

Chapter 5: Integrating DBT into Everyday Life

Incorporating DBT Principles into Relationships and Work

Incorporating Dialectical Behavior Therapy (DBT) principles into relationships and work environments can lead to improved communication, collaboration, and overall well-being. Here's how DBT principles can be applied in these contexts:

Relationships:

Mindful Communication:

DBT Principle: Mindfulness is crucial in DBT, and it can enhance communication by promoting active listening and non-judgmental awareness.

Application: Practice being fully present in conversations. Listen actively without interrupting, and respond mindfully rather than reactively. This fosters understanding and connection.

Emotional Regulation:

DBT Principle: Recognize and manage intense emotions without impulsive reactions.

Application: In conflicts, take a moment to identify and validate your emotions. Communicate your feelings assertively and constructively, avoiding blame or criticism. Encourage your partner to express themselves similarly.

Interpersonal Effectiveness:

DBT Principle: Learn effective communication skills and assertiveness to navigate relationships.

Application: Clearly express your needs, set boundaries, and negotiate compromises when necessary. Use "DEAR MAN" (Describe, Express, Assert, Reinforce, Mindful, Appear confident, Negotiate) skills to communicate more effectively.

Validation:

DBT Principle: Validate your own and others' experiences and emotions.

Application: Practice acknowledging and validating your partner's feelings, even if you may not fully understand them. This fosters a supportive environment and strengthens the emotional connection in the relationship.

Wise Mind in Decision-Making:

DBT Principle: Integrate emotional and rational thinking to make balanced decisions.

Application: When making decisions together, consider both emotional and logical aspects. Strive for a "wise mind" approach that aligns with shared values and long-term goals, minimizing impulsive reactions.

Work:

Mindful Work Practices:

DBT Principle: Mindfulness can reduce stress and improve focus.

Application: Incorporate mindfulness practices into your work routine. Take short breaks for mindful breathing, practice staying fully engaged in tasks, and approach challenges with a non-judgmental mindset.

Emotional Regulation in the Workplace:

DBT Principle: Manage emotions effectively to prevent impulsive reactions.

Application: When faced with stressors at work, take a moment to identify and regulate your emotions. Avoid impulsive responses and consider constructive ways to address challenges, fostering a more positive work environment.

Interpersonal Effectiveness in Teamwork:

DBT Principle: Apply effective communication and collaboration skills.

Application: Clearly communicate your ideas, actively listen to others, and provide constructive feedback. Use interpersonal effectiveness skills to navigate workplace dynamics, fostering a more cohesive and productive team.

Distress Tolerance in High-Pressure Situations:

DBT Principle: Develop resilience to withstand crises without making impulsive decisions.

Application: When facing high-pressure situations, practice distress tolerance. Identify healthy coping mechanisms, seek support when needed, and avoid impulsive actions that could have negative consequences in the long run.

Validation in the Workplace:

DBT Principle: Acknowledge and validate your own and others' experiences.

Application: Recognize and appreciate the contributions of your colleagues. Provide positive feedback and acknowledgment for a job well done. Creating a validating workplace culture enhances motivation and job satisfaction.

In both relationships and work settings, the key is to consistently apply and practice these principles. DBT skills can contribute to healthier communication, emotional regulation, and decision-making, ultimately fostering more positive and constructive interactions in various aspects of life. If challenges persist, seeking support from a mental health professional trained in DBT can provide additional guidance and assistance.

Integrating DBT Skills for Recharged Living: Mind, Body, and Sleep

Getting enough sleep is essential for maintaining your general health and wellbeing. A healthy sleep schedule can boost your immune system, lower your risk of diabetes, lower your chance of heart disease, and increase your focus and productivity.

Nonetheless, one in three Americans do not get enough sleep. According to estimates, between 50 and 70 million Americans suffer from a sleep disorder, and between 9 and 15% claim that their day-to-day activities are negatively impacted by sleep deprivation.

By addressing the underlying cause of your sleep-related problems, dialectical behavior therapy, or DBT, can help you get a better night's sleep. DBT may be able to assist you in creating a sleep schedule and in returning to sleep following a nightmare. This is especially crucial if you have trouble falling asleep at night because even small adjustments to your nighttime routine can have a significant impact.

SIGNS OF POOR SLEEP

Your mental health and general well-being can suffer greatly from poor sleep quality. However, if you are not aware of subtle indicators such as these, it can be challenging to recognize the signs of poor sleep: Dry mouth or sore throat; Jaw and tooth pain; New pimples and acne outbreaks; Abrupt mood swings and anxiety; Junk food and coffee cravings.

All of these signs suggest that your sleep was not very good. Your jaw pain and dry mouth are signs that you probably have sleep apnea. Sleep apnea is characterized by breathing pauses that leave your mouth dry and sore in the morning.

Brain fog can also occur if you have trouble getting enough sleep. A disturbed night's sleep can cause difficulty concentrating because the brain becomes easily overworked. Additionally, this may deplete your energy and make you feel unnecessarily nervous or grumpy.

SLEEP HYGIENE

Your physical and emotional well-being are greatly impacted by the quantity and quality of your sleep. However, if you've had sleep problems for a while, you might not know where to start.

By establishing a schedule for you to adhere to, DBT can raise the possibility that you will get a good night's sleep. You can control your emotional reaction to sleep—or lack thereof—with the aid of this routine. This is especially beneficial if you experience anxiety before bed. When adhering to a DBT program, you can employ methods such as: 9 to 0 meditation; body scans; comfort and positive self-talk.

Make an effort to keep your room cool, and use your bed just for sleeping. This can create a strong, positive association between your bed and sleep time and help you fall asleep a little faster.

If you can't sleep at all, think about getting up and doing some simple tasks instead of lying awake all night. You can sleep better as well if you can learn to listen to your body. You may not need 8 hours of sleep and could find it stressful to force yourself to get more shut-eye than necessary.

NIGHTMARE

In most cases, nightmares are not cause for concern and are a rather common occurrence. However, you might want to seek the assistance of a DBT specialist if nightmares are making it difficult for you to fall asleep.

The goal of the DBT nightmare protocol is to give you mastery over your dreams. You have the power to control your imagination and to alter how you feel while you sleep. Begin by engaging in self-soothing and relaxation exercises as coping mechanisms. After you've gained some resilience, think about working with a professional to address a traumatic nightmare.

You can begin treating recurrent nightmares by jotting down the details of the dream and selecting a different resolution. Please ensure that this change takes place prior to any negative events, and feel free to utilize your imagination to create other changes.

ANXIETY RELIEF

You can better understand the cause of your insomnia and get more rest by consulting with a sleep specialist. If you want to truly maximize your time in bed, you'll still need to deal with stress. Before going to bed, think about a few simple stress-reduction techniques, such as:

guided imagery, progressive muscle relaxation, and belly breathing.

If you do experience a poor night's sleep, don't worry about it. Rather, concentrate on making changes to feel more energized throughout the day. Think about, for instance: Eating a lot of vegetables and high-quality proteins; scheduling exercise when you're feeling tired; drinking plenty of water; and giving up alcohol.

These easy steps can help reduce your stress related to sleep and increase your energy levels. See a DBT specialist as a follow-up to address the underlying cause of your sleep problems.

You can enhance the quality of your sleep with DBT. DBT should first be incorporated into your sleep schedule. This can help you deal with nightmares that keep coming back and help you fall asleep. Try some methods like belly breathing, body scans, and guided meditations if you're still having trouble.

6

Chapter 6: Implementing DBT in your counseling practice

When it comes to implementation and training, counselors who want to incorporate DBT into their own practice frequently find it difficult to know where to start. Complete, "standard" DBT implementation can be expensive and time-consuming. It also has the strongest body of evidence, which raises the probability and potency of favorable results.

Conversely, counselors might be more interested in implementing specific DBT techniques (like the skills training group) or changing the existing skills curriculum and headshot handouts. This type of treatment has been called "DBT-informed," and depending on the population and environment the counselor is working with, it may also be helpful. Basic considerations for counselors considering the use of standard or DBT-informed practices are covered in this article.

The four DBT modes

In DBT, there are various treatment modalities to take into account, each of which addresses one or more particular functions of the standard model. These are the four common modes of DBT treatment, though Linehan notes that additional ancillary modes (like medication and case management) may be used.

1) Skills training: Due to its tangible handouts and instructions for group leaders, the DBT skills group is one of the most widely used DBT implementations. It also often requires the fewest resources. There is also a substantial body of research supporting the efficacy of addressing a range of treatment objectives and mental health symptoms solely through skills training. The experience of skill training is organized and has a psychoeducational focus. In this DBT approach, clients only work on developing new skills, improving their capacities, and applying new skills to other areas of their lives. The four skill modules are: interpersonal effectiveness, emotion regulation, distress tolerance, and mindfulness.

Individual sessions can be used to finish skill training. But as Linehan points out in the DBT Skills Training Manual, it can be challenging for the therapist to set guidelines and schedule skill-building time within the therapeutic session. Group sessions are therefore typically the recommended approach. Weekly sessions lasting two to two and a half hours are customary in group settings. While the second hour is spent learning new skills, the first hour is spent reviewing homework from the previous session.

Usually, the modules last between five and seven weeks. But, depending on the requirements of the website and the customers, the duration and format may be changed. For instance, group sessions could be offered more frequently than once a week or within a shorter time frame. Linehan adds that while groups can be closed or open, open groups appear to be the most advantageous when it comes to developing skills. In my experience, when a new module started, I (Michelle) closed the group and then welcomed new members when the next module started. Members of the group were able to collaborate and study throughout each module as a result.

2) Phone coaching: It's common knowledge that the most rigorous type of traditional DBT is intake phone coaching. This makes sense since counselors may prefer to devote all of their attention to their families and personal time when they are not working, as they spend a great deal of energy being there for their clients during regularly scheduled sessions. Counselors may also be concerned about their clients abusing their availability to them at any time after hours, particularly if they have a history of urgent needs.

But in order to assist clients in applying the skills they have acquired in training to their daily lives, Linehan has stressed the value of intersession coaching. A skills coaching call lasts for about ten to twenty minutes, on average. Linehan and her colleagues point out that although the frequency of calls will differ per client, it should decrease as more time is spent in the program.

Regarding the use of phone calls for skills coaching in between sessions, a number of guidelines are provided. This framework encourages the client to use their skills rather than resorting to needless hospital stays or life-threatening behaviors (such as nonsuicidal self-injury). According to Linehan, skills coaching sessions with nurses, mental health technicians, and other staff members can replace conventional phone coaching if DBT is used in an inpatient or residential setting.

3) Therapist consultation team: Linehan and associates stress the significance of providing therapists with support. The consultation team is made up of DBT-trained therapists who get together once a week to discuss cases, offer support, and ensure treatment fidelity. Counselors who are thinking about applying DBT at their current sites have two options: they can approach an existing DBT consultation team in the community or form a new consultation

team.

It can be challenging to join a DBT team, particularly in rural areas. Linehan does point out that if needed, team members can schedule weekly meetings using internet resources. Linehan and her colleagues advise designating a team leader for individuals forming a new team on-site. A capable team leader offers direction and keeps the group motivated and focused during the course of the treatment. In addition, this individual will be useful in assigning team members to different roles according to their skills, experiences, and areas of interest. The role of the consultation team in standard DBT is to improve the skills and motivation of therapists.

4) Individual treatment: Weekly individual treatment under standard DBT focuses primarily on increasing the client's motivation. A skills trainer and an individual counselor are typically not the same. Since group therapy sessions are more psychoeducational in nature, individual therapy also provides a safe space for the client to process suicidal thoughts and nonsuicidal self-injury. In addition to a behavioral approach to quality-of-life, life-threatening, and therapy-interfering behaviors, the individual therapist in standard DBT employs dialectical and validation treatment strategies, per Linehan's original text on treating borderline personality disorder.

General things to think about

Counselors should take into account a number of other factors before implementing DBT in addition to the modes. Where DBT can be successfully incorporated into current systems will be determined by conducting an initial needs assessment. This includes evaluating the target population and the human and non-human resources that are available for the course of treatment. Important things to think about are:

Population: Research has indicated that DBT can be helpful for adults and adolescents with eating disorders, mood disorders, anxiety disorders, and substance use disorders, even though it was first designed for adults with borderline personality disorder. Program development and execution will be grounded by focusing only on the target population. In addition to any potential client exclusions or exceptions, admission requirements are a crucial factor to take into account. Admission of clients need not always be restricted or wide. It should, nevertheless, be constant. It is imperative for counselors to take into account how the selected population addresses the gaps in the community's current services, such as the availability of eating disorder clinics, chemical dependency treatment facilities, and ongoing community support groups. It is also advisable to think about any modifications that might need to be made to the skill worksheets and handouts. There are numerous publications by Linehan and other experts that discuss adjustments to meet the requirements of particular age groups and diagnoses.

Training: Counselors interested in DBT have access to a wide range of training options. Many people believe that Behavioral Tech, the company that Linehan founded to train others and support DBT research, provides the best DBT training available. Counselors can apply the skills they learn in the first 10-day intensive course to their practices; however, it is restricted to treatment teams. This course can be taken in five days as an abridged version for counselors who want to join an existing DBT team. For providers who have been using DBT for a year or longer, Behavioral Tech offers advanced intensive training in addition to online resources and additional training materials for individuals. Recently, Linehan and associates started providing an official DBT certification. To become certified, one must complete at least 40 hours of DBT-related training, pass the certification exam, and submit a client case conceptualization that includes three taped sessions.

Individuals across the nation can attend a variety of local and regional DBT trainings provided by other organizations. There are also numerous textual and online resources available. When selecting the ideal training location, finances and the planned extent of DBT implementation are both crucial factors to take into account. All counselors and other staff members involved must have a solid foundation in DBT before proceeding, regardless of the type or level of training they choose.

Setting and facilities: Decisions about the adaptation and application of DBT will be heavily influenced by the setting. To deliver DBT in less time, clinicians in intensive outpatient or inpatient settings might need to make major adjustments. Institutions that cater exclusively to particular demographics might require highly specialized skill and treatment modality adaptations.

Additional important considerations are space and other on-site resources. Depending on the anticipated number of clients and, if relevant, the quantity and frequency of groups being implemented, needs may differ. Ideally, there will be sufficient room for all counselors and staff members to work comfortably. It is imperative to contemplate the provision of specific on-site amenities, such as a lending library, designated areas for other professionals and paraprofessionals, and a private respite area for clinicians. It is crucial to examine the advantages and disadvantages of each of these factors.

Finances and billing: When training, resources, and time are taken into account, a full implementation of standard DBT can be expensive. However, because DBT results in fewer emergency hospitalizations, Linehan and her colleagues have discovered that DBT is frequently more cost-effective for the community than "treatment as usual" with chronically suicidal individuals. All DBT modes may, however, be challenging to get reimbursed for, particularly for practitioners who work in private practices. According to DBT researchers, community mental health centers might be the most suitable choice for putting full DBT into practice because they frequently bill Medicaid and Medicare, which might be more accommodating when it comes to session limits and treatment reimbursement. Selecting which DBT modes to use and for how long requires doing a cost-benefit analysis.

Evaluation of the program and assessment: Linehan and her associates have always underlined that an essential component of any DBT program is assessment. No matter how DBT is implemented or modified, it is critical that all parties involved are aware of the results that clients achieve. Early on in the implementation process, it is important to clearly identify the symptoms or behaviors that the program will address and to decide how to assess participants using psychometric tests and other techniques. The DBT Skills Training Manual contains a list of various options for assessment tools that Linehan offers.

Administrative and structural support: DBT researchers have discovered that the time and resources required by administrators is one of the main barriers to DBT implementation. Administrators might not be aware of the evidence supporting the use of all DBT modalities or the comprehensive nature of the treatment. Counselors should present this information to administrators at first and highlight the treatment's advantages according to recently released research.

Support for counselors using DBT and agency structure are also crucial factors to take into account. Counselors must decide whether to work with DBT-focused cases exclusively or to handle a variety of case types. A full-time caseload with standard DBT can vary, but typically consists of 14–18 clients. This makes time for skills groups, individual sessions, weekly phone consultations (15–30 minutes per client), and paperwork possible.

Treatment duration and modifications: Standard DBT calls for a client and counselor to invest time and energy. Effective treatment for borderline personality disorder is likely to be intensive because the majority of patients have previously received long-term mental health services. Pretreatment therapy commitment is essential and frequently involves a cooperative agreement between the client and the counselor. This initial commitment usually lasts between six and a year (clients should ideally complete two six-month cycles of skills training). This timeline may be extended, but in order to avoid treatment dependency or deception, the terms of the extension, such as its duration and expectations, should be made clear. It's also beneficial to have standard procedures for determining what makes a successful graduation and how to celebrate the milestone.

Advantages and drawbacks of using DBT

The advantages and drawbacks of implementing standard DBT or DBT-informed treatment at your agency or practice are discussed in the following section.

Advantages of Standard DBT

- Evidence-based and highly structured, standard DBT is an intervention. Because counselors, administrators, other service providers, and clients will know exactly what will be included and the protocol that will be followed, this can actually make implementation easier.
- When attempting to obtain grant money for programs, funders may find DBT appealing due to its evidence-based approach. Keep in mind that funders are more likely to do this if they are aware of the benefits of DBT, which include lower treatment costs overall, fewer hospitalizations, and a decline in both non-suicidal self-injury and suicide attempts.
- The main goals of DBT treatment are addressed by each mode, which includes boosting capacities, maintaining treatment providers' skills and motivation, guaranteeing generalization, improving motivation, and improving environments.
- Standard DBT is the foundation of the vast majority of studies on the efficacy of DBT.

Limitations of Standard DBT

- For certain agencies and practitioners, the expenses associated with comprehensive training and the requirement for a team to execute the plan may be unaffordable.

- For DBT to be implemented successfully, practitioners must have a strong commitment to the technique. Respecting the model entails acknowledging the fundamental tenets of treatment:

1) making life worthwhile for clients

2) thinking that clients can get better by learning to meet their needs in more functional and adaptive ways

3) understanding that DBT carries some inherent risk due to the client's typically erratic emotional states and suicidal thoughts and behaviors at the beginning of treatment.

- It can be expensive to implement all DBT modalities, and counselors may have trouble billing insurance companies for standard DBT. Counselors may also need to devote a substantial amount of time to it, including staying up late to conduct the necessary phone consultations with clients.

Advantages of DBT-informed care

- Clients with a wide range of presenting problems, such as anxiety, adjustment disorders, stress, and decision-making issues, can benefit from the skills taught in the four DBT modules. For instance, because this module covers how to uphold relationships, make requests and say no, and maintain self-respect in relationships, interpersonal effectiveness skills can be used with social skills groups.
- The majority of the research indicates that implementing DBT partially is effective. Specifically, it supports the use of either a skills group alone

or in conjunction with one or more other treatment modalities.

- For both clients and counselors, it might be more economical to implement specific DBT modifications or components.
- A modified version of DBT that incorporates some modes only partially can give administrators, counselors, and clients more flexibility.

Restrictions on DBT-informed therapy

- Research on the efficacy of partial DBT implementation is still lacking, despite its support. Furthermore, more investigation is required into the particular DBT components that are most beneficial in terms of treatment goals.
- People who are adopting DBT will find it more challenging to organize their care and make sure that every aspect of the treatment is covered without using all four of the standard modes.
- Counselors may need to make their own resources in order to meet the needs of their clients, as there are fewer resources available for those who want to modify the techniques and handouts for particular diagnoses.

7

Chapter 7: Overcoming Challenges in DBT

Common Roadblocks and How to Navigate Them

Similar to any other therapeutic approach or personal development program, there are typical obstacles that people may run into when attempting to apply Dialectical Behavior Therapy (DBT) techniques in their daily lives. The following are a few of these obstacles and how to get around them:

1. Resistance to Change:

Obstacle: Individuals may be reluctant to embrace novel actions or perspectives, particularly if they are deeply rooted.

Navigational Approach: Set reasonable objectives and start small. Integrate DBT techniques into your daily practice gradually. To increase confidence and motivation, acknowledge even small successes. Accept that change is a process, and practice self-compassion.

2. Lack of Regularity:

Obstacle: The efficacy of DBT skills can be impeded by inconsistent practice.

Navigational Approach: Create a schedule for practicing your skills. Make it a habit to incorporate and practice DBT skills into your daily routine. Reminders can be programmed in or added to ongoing tasks. For skills to be developed and integrated into daily life, consistency is essential.

3. Complicated Transferring Knowledge:

Obstacle: Using DBT techniques in a variety of contexts can be difficult.

Navigational Approach: Practice your generalization skills in a variety of situations to improve them. Find recurring themes or patterns in your life where you can use particular abilities. Consider how you can adjust and change your skills to suit different circumstances. Generalization is improved by regular practice in a variety of situations.

4. Too Much Emotional Overload:

Obstacle: People may become overwhelmed by strong emotions, which makes it challenging to use DBT techniques when needed.

Navigational Approach: Gain the ability to tolerate discomfort in order to control intense feelings. Engage in self-soothing activities such as deep breathing exercises and grounding techniques. Recall that when emotions are more under control, it's acceptable to step back and resume problem-solving.

5. Adverse Self-Talk:

Obstacle: Self-criticism and negative self-talk can sabotage attempts to use DBT techniques.

Navigational Approach: Develop self-compassion and self-validation. Use cognitive restructuring strategies to refute negative ideas. A more balanced and upbeat affirmation should take the place of self-critical thoughts. Establishing a constructive internal dialogue is crucial for long-term development.

6. Lack of Social Support:

Obstacle: It can be difficult to apply DBT techniques successfully if there is a lack of social support.

Navigational Approach: Ask friends, family, or support groups for social support. Tell a trusted person about your objectives and request support and responsibility. Take part in activities that build relationships and encourage teamwork to create a positive social atmosphere.

7. Time-related perception:

Obstacle: An impression that there isn't enough time for DBT skill practice may result from hectic schedules.

Navigational Approach: Make skill practice and self-care a priority. Divide skills into doable steps that you can incorporate into your daily routine. Think about the long-term advantages of devoting time to your health. Over time, even brief, consistent practice sessions can have a big impact.

8. Fear of Failure:

Obstacle: It can be extremely crippling to be afraid of failing or making mistakes.

Navigational Approach: Adopt a growth mentality. Consider obstacles as chances for growth and development as opposed to setbacks. Recognize that obstacles are an inevitable aspect of learning. Honor the work you've done to make improvements.

9. Lack of Professional Guidance:

Obstacle: People may find it difficult to comprehend and implement DBT concepts in their daily lives without the assistance of a professional.

Navigation Strategy: You might want to think about seeing a DBT-trained mental health professional for therapy. They are able to offer tailored advice, encouragement, and criticism. Additionally, group therapy settings may present chances to pick up and hone skills in a welcoming environment.

10. Not Adapting to Individual Needs:

Obstacle: Applying a general strategy might not be able to accommodate different people's preferences and needs.

Navigation Strategy: Adapt DBT techniques to your unique situation and inclinations. Try out a variety of skill variations to see which one suits you the best. Be adaptable and willing to modify the principles to fit your particular personality and circumstances.

Overcoming these obstacles calls for self-awareness, dedication, and a readiness to change and advance. It's critical to approach the procedure patiently and acknowledge that obstacles are a necessary part of the process. Seeking advice from a mental health professional can offer invaluable support and help in overcoming obstacles if problems continue.

Adjusting DBT for Individual Needs

The comprehensive and adaptable approach of dialectical behavior therapy (DBT) can be tailored to each person's needs. Although borderline personality disorder was the original reason for its development, a wide range of people and mental health issues can benefit from its concepts and abilities. Here's how to modify DBT to meet the needs of each individual:

1. Customizing the Selection of Skills: Modification: Acknowledge that not every DBT skill will be applicable to every situation. Make sure the skills you choose are appropriate for your needs, preferences, and particular challenges. For instance, a person who has trouble controlling their emotions might give priority to DBT skills associated with that area.

2. Tailoring Skill Utilization: Modification: Adjust the application of skills to fit the preferences and lifestyles of individuals. If someone finds that formal mindfulness meditation isn't for them, they could try other mindfulness exercises like mindful breathing or mindful walking.

3. Modifying Mindfulness Practices: Although mindfulness is an essential part of DBT, various people may find different mindfulness exercises to be effective. Encourage the person to try out different methods until they discover the one that suits them the best. This could include guided meditations, mindfulness applications, or even creative pursuits like gardening or painting.

4. Flexible Diary Card Implementation: Modification: Although diary cards are frequently used in DBT to track behaviors, emotions, and skill usage, the format can be changed to suit personal preferences. While some might benefit from a more thorough and imaginative approach, others might prefer a digital format or a more condensed version.

5. Customized Objectives and Goals: Modification: Establish personalized treatment objectives and targets in collaboration. Concentrate on the particular facets of life that the person wishes to enhance. Relationships, employment, self-worth, and other individual goals that are pertinent to their well-being may be examples of this.

6. Adaptable Timing and Frequency: Modification Modify the duration and frequency of skill practice sessions and therapy sessions to accommodate each person's schedule and obligations. While some people might benefit from checking in more frequently, others might prefer to wait longer between sessions.

7. Integration with Other Therapeutic Approaches: Modification: Depending on the needs of each patient, DBT can be combined with other therapeutic modalities. For example, cognitive-behavioral therapy (CBT) components that are customized to address particular anxiety triggers may be beneficial for an individual undergoing DBT for anxiety.

8. Cultural Sensitivity: Adjustment: When applying DBT, take cultural considerations into account. Make sure the exercises, examples, and language used are appropriate for the target culture. This could entail changing some

DBT components to better fit with societal norms and values.

9. Adapting to Different Learning Styles: Modification: Acknowledge and make accommodations for various learning styles. Some people might learn better with visual aids, while others might benefit more from spoken explanations or practical exercises. Modify the delivery method to improve comprehension and involvement.

10. Modifying Homework Assignments: Modify assignments to take into account unique situations. Recognize the person's abilities and way of life when assigning tasks, and make sure they are difficult but doable. This makes it possible to guarantee that skill practice continues outside of therapy sessions.

11. Encouraging Gradual Advancement: Modification: Recognize that advancement is frequently gradual and can differ amongst people. Recognize and celebrate minor successes as a way to emphasize the value of persistent work over time.

12. Using Technology: Modification: Make use of technology to improve the way DBT techniques are applied. This could involve using apps, online resources, or virtual therapy sessions to accommodate individual preferences and accessibility.

13. Input and Cooperation: Modification: Promote candid dialogue between the patient and the therapist. Seek input on how well the strategy is working on a regular basis, and be willing to make changes in response to the person's changing needs and objectives.

In order to tailor DBT to each person's needs, the therapist and the client must work together and be adaptable. In order to make sure that the treatment plan is in line with each patient's particular situation and promotes significant advancement toward their objective, it is crucial to regularly evaluate and modify it.

8

Appreciation

As I pen down these final words of this book, I find it fitting to express my heartfelt gratitude to you for taking the time to read these pages. Your support and interest in this work mean the world to me.

Writing a book is a journey of passion, creativity, and perseverance, but it wouldn't have the same meaning without readers like you. You've chosen to embark on this literary adventure, and for that, I am truly thankful.

I hope that within these pages, you've found inspiration, knowledge, or perhaps just what you were looking for. Books have the remarkable ability to transport us, teach us, and connect us with new ideas and perspectives. I sincerely hope that this book has fulfilled some of these roles for you.

The act of writing is solitary, but the act of reading is communal. In reading, we share a unique bond, and it's your engagement with the words on these pages that breathes life into the ideas contained within.

I also want to extend my appreciation to you for offering feedback, support, and encouragement along this journey. If you have not given this book a review on Amazon.com, please show some support.

Remember that the power of books lies not only in their pages but in the Values and reflections they inspire. So, whether you loved the book or found areas for improvement, your thoughts and opinions matter, and I'm grateful for them.

Thank you, dear reader, for being a part of this literary journey. I'm immensely thankful for your time, attention, and support.